THE METHOD OF GRACE

THE METHOD
OF GRACE

A SERMON PREACHED ON SABBATH MORNING, SEPT. 13TH, 1741, IN THE HIGH-CHURCH-YARD OF GLASGOW

BY THE

REV. GEORGE WHITEFIELD, M.A.

LATE OF PEMBROKE COLLEGE, OXFORD, AND CHAPLAIN TO THE RIGHT HONORABLE THE COUNTESS OF HUNTINGDON

CURIOSMITH

MINNEAPOLIS

2012

Published by Curiosmith.
P. O. Box 390293, Minneapolis, Minnesota, 55439.
Internet: curiosmith.com.
E-mail: shopkeeper@curiosmith.com.

Previously published—Glasgow: Printed, and sold by Robert Smith, 1741.

The text of this edition is from *Memoirs of Reverend George Whitefield* by John Gillies, D. D. Middletown: Hunt & Co., 1841.

The Outline of the Contents was added to this edition by the publisher.

Supplementary content and cover design:
Copyright © 2012 Charles J. Doe.

ISBN 9781935626602

OUTLINE OF THE CONTENTS

The Method of Grace

A SERMON BY

George Whitefield, M.A.

They have healed also the hurt of the daughter of my people slightly, saying, peace, peace, when there is no peace.
—JEREMIAH 6:14.

A s God can send a nation or people no greater blessing, than to give them faithful, sincere, and upright ministers; so the greatest curse that God can possibly send upon a people in this world, is to give them over to blind, unregenerate, carnal, lukewarm, and unskillful guides. And yet, in all ages, we find that there have been many wolves in sheep's clothing, many that daubed with untempered mortar, that prophesied smoother things than God did allow. As it was formerly, so it is now, there are many that corrupt the word of God, and deal deceitfully with it. It was so in a special manner in the prophet Jeremiah's time; and he, faithful to that God that employed, him, did not fail, from time to time, to open his mouth against them, and to bear a noble testimony to the honor of that God, in whose name he from time to time spake. If you will read his prophecy, you will find, that none spake more against such ministers than Jeremiah: and here especially, in the chapter out of which the text is taken, he speaks very severely against them; he charges them with several crimes, particularly, he charges them with covetousness: for, says he in the 13th verse, "from the least of them even to the greatest of them, every one is given to covetousness; and from the prophet even unto the priest, every one dealeth falsely." And then in the words of the text, in a more special manner, he exemplifies how they had dealt falsely, how they had behaved treacherously to poor souls, says he, *they have healed also the hurt of the daughter of my people slightly, saying peace, peace, when there is no peace.* The prophet, in the name of God, had been denouncing war against the people, he had been telling them, that their houses should be left desolate, and the Lord would certainly visit the land with war, "therefore," says he, in the 11th verse, "I am full of the fury of the Lord: I am weary with holding in: I will pour it out upon the children abroad, and upon the assembly of young men together. For even the husband with the wife shall be taken, the aged with him that is full of days. And their houses shall be turned unto others, with their fields and wives together: for I will stretch out my hand upon the inhabitants of the land, saith the Lord." The prophet gives a thundering message, that they might be terrified, and have some convictions and inclinations to repent: but it seems that the false prophets, the false priests, went about stifling people's convictions, and when they were hurt or a little terrified, they were for daubing over the wound, telling them, that Jeremiah was but an enthusiastic preacher; that there could be no such thing as a war among them; and bidding people "peace, peace, be still," when the prophet told them there was no peace. The words then refer primarily unto outward things; but I verily believe have also a further reference to the soul; and are to be referred to those false teachers, who, when people were under conviction of sin, when people were beginning to look towards heaven, were for stifling their convictions, and telling them they were good enough before. And indeed people generally love to have it so: our hearts are exceedingly deceitful and desperately wicked; none but the eternal God knows how treacherous they are. How many of us cry, peace, peace, to our souls, when there is no peace. How many are there that are now settled upon their lees, that now think they are Christians, that now flatter themselves that they have an interest in Jesus Christ; whereas if we come to examine their experiences, we will find that their peace is but a peace of the devil's making; it is not a peace of God's giving; it is not a peace that passeth human understanding. It is matter therefore of great importance, my dear hearers, to know whether we may speak peace to our hearts. We are all desirous of peace, peace is an unspeakable blessing. How can we live without peace? And therefore people, from time to time, must be taught how far they must go, and what must be wrought in them, before they can speak peace to their hearts. This is what I design at present, that I may deliver my soul, that I may be free from the blood of all those to whom I preach, that I may not fail to declare the whole counsel of God. I shall from the words of the text, endeavor to show you what you must undergo, and what must be wrought in you, before ye can speak peace to your hearts.

But before I come directly to this, give me leave to premise a caution or two. And the first is, that I take it for granted ye believe religion to be an inward thing; ye believe it to be a work in the heart, a work wrought in the soul by the power of the Spirit of God. If you do not believe this, ye do not believe your Bible. If ye do not believe this, though ye have got your Bible in your hands, ye hate the Lord Jesus Christ in your heart: for religion is every where represented in scripture, as the work of God in the heart; "the kingdom of God is within us," says our Lord; and, "he is not a Christian that is one outwardly, but he is a Christian who is one inwardly." If any of you place religion in outward things, I shall not perhaps please you this morning; ye will understand me no more when I speak of the work of God upon a poor sinner's heart, than if I were talking in an unknown tongue. I would further premise a caution, that I would by no means confine God to one way of acting; I would by no means say, that all persons before they come to have a settled peace in their hearts, are obliged to undergo the same degrees of conviction. No; God has various ways of bringing his children home; his sacred spirit bloweth when, and where, and how, it listeth. But however, I will venture to affirm this, that before ever ye can speak peace to your hearts, whether by shorter or longer continuance of your convictions, whether in a more pungent or in a more gentle way, ye must undergo what I shall hereafter lay down in the following discourse.

First, Then, before ye can speak peace to your hearts, ye must be made to see, made to feel, made to weep over, made to bewail your actual transgressions against the law of God. According to the covenant of works, the soul that sinneth it shall die; cursed is that man, be what he will, be who he will, that continueth not in all things that are written in the book of the law to do them. We are not only to do some things, but we are to do all things, and we are to continue so to do; so that the least deviation from the moral law, according to the covenant of works, whether in thought, word, or deed, deserves eternal death at the hand of God. And if one evil thought, if one evil word, if one evil action, deserves eternal damnation; how many hells, my friends, do every one of us deserve, whose whole lives have been one continual rebellion against God. Before ever therefore ye can speak peace to your hearts, ye must be brought to see, brought to believe, what a dreadful thing it is to depart from the living God. And now, my dear friends, examine your hearts, for I hope ye come hither with a design to have your souls made better: give me leave to ask you, in the presence of God, whether ye know the time, and if ye do not know exactly the time, do ye know there was a time when God wrote bitter things against you, when the arrows of the Almighty were within you? Was ever the remembrance of your sins grievous to you? Was the burden of your sins intolerable to your thoughts? Did ye ever see that God's wrath might justly fall upon you, upon account of your actual transgressions against God? Were ye ever in all your life sorry for your sins? Could ye ever say, my sins are gone over my head as a burden too heavy for me to bear? Did ye ever experience any such thing as this? Did ever any such thing as this pass between God and your soul? If not, for Jesus Christ's sake do not call yourselves Christians; ye may speak peace to your hearts, but there is no peace. May the Lord awaken you, may the Lord convert you, may the Lord give you peace, if it be his will, before you go home.

But further, ye may be convinced of your actual sins, so as to be made to tremble, and yet ye may be strangers to Jesus Christ, ye may have no true work of grace upon your heart. Before ever, therefore, ye can speak peace to your hearts, conviction must go deeper; ye must not only be convinced of your actual transgressions against the law of God, but likewise of the foundation of all your transgressions; and what is that? I mean original sin; that original corruption each of us brings into the world with us, which renders us liable to God's wrath and damnation. There are many poor souls that think themselves fine reasoners, yet they pretend to say there is no such thing as original sin; they will charge God with injustice in imputing Adam's sin to us; although we have got the mark of the beast, and of the devil upon us, yet they tell us, we are not born in sin. Let them look abroad in the world, and see the disorders in it, and think if they can, if this is the paradise in which God did put man? No, every thing in the world is out of order. I have often thought, when I was abroad, that if there were no other argument to prove original sin, but the rising of wolves and tigers against man, nay, the barking of a dog against us, is a proof of original sin. Tigers and lions durst not rise against us, if it were not for Adam's first sin: for when the creatures rise up against us, it is as much as to say, ye have sinned against God, and we take up our masters quarrel. If we look inward, we will see enough of lusts, and man's temper contrary to the temper of God; there is pride, malice, and revenge in all our hearts, and this temper cannot come from God; it comes from our first parent, Adam, who, after he fell from God, fell out of God into the devil. However, therefore, some people may deny this, yet when conviction comes, all carnal reasonings are battered down immediately, and the poor soul begins to feel and see the fountain from which all the polluted streams do flow. When the sinner is first awakened, he begins to wonder how he came to be so wicked: the Spirit of God then strikes in, and shows that he has no good thing in him by nature; then he sees that he is altogether gone out of the way; that he is altogether become abominable; and the poor creature is made to lie down at the foot of the throne of God, and to acknowledge that God would be just to damn him, just to cut him off, though he never had committed one actual sin in his life. Did ye ever feel and experience this any of you, to justify God in your damnation; to own that ye are by nature children of wrath, and that God may justly cut you off though ye never actually had offended him in all your life. If ye were ever truly convicted—if your hearts were ever truly cut—if self were truly taken out of you, ye will be made to see and feel this. And if ye have never felt the weight of original sin, do not call yourselves Christians. I am verily persuaded original sin is the greatest burden of a true convert; this even grieves the regenerate soul—the sanctified soul. The indwelling of sin in the heart is the burden of a converted person; it is the burden of a true Christian; he continually cries out, O "Who will deliver me from this body of death," this indwelling corruption of my heart; this is that which disturbs a poor soul most. And, therefore, if ye never felt this inward corruption—if ye never saw that God might justly curse you for it; indeed, my dear friends, ye may speak peace to your heart, but I fear, nay, I know, there is no true peace.

Further, before we can speak peace to your hearts, ye must not only be troubled for the sins of your life, the sins of your nature, but likewise for the sins of your best duties and performances. When a poor soul is somewhat awakened by the terrors of the Lord, then the poor creature, being born under the covenant of works flies directly to a covenant of works again. And as Adam and Eve hid themselves among the trees of the garden, and sewed fig-leaves together to covet their nakedness; so the poor sinner when awakened, flies to his duties, and to his performances, to hide himself from God; and goes to patch up a righteousness of his own; says he, I will be mighty good now; I will reform, I will do all I can and then certainly Jesus Christ will have mercy on me. But before ye can speak peace to your heart, ye must be brought to see that God may justly damn you for the best prayer ye ever put up in all your life; ye must be brought to see all your duties, all your righteousness, as the prophet elegantly expresses it, put them altogether, are so far from recommending you to God, are so far from being any motive and inducement to God to have mercy on your poor souls, that ye will see them to be filthy rags, a menstruous cloth; that God hates them, and cannot away with them, if ye bring them to him in order to recommend you to his favor. My dear friends, what is there in our performances to recommend us unto God; our persons are in an unsanctified state by nature, we deserve to be damned ten thousand times over; and what must our performances be? We can do no good thing by nature; "they that are in the flesh cannot please God." Ye may do things materially good, but ye cannot do a thing formally and rightly good; because nature cannot act above itself. It is impossible that a man that is unconverted can act for the glory of God; he cannot do any thing in faith, for "whatsoever is not of faith is sin." After we are renewed, yet we are renewed but in part; indwelling sin continues in us; there is a mixture of corruption in every one of our duties; so that after we are converted, were Jesus Christ only to accept us according to our works, our works would damn us; for we cannot put up a prayer but it is far from that perfection which the moral law requireth. I do not know what ye may think; but I can say that I cannot pray but I sin; I cannot preach to you or any others but I sin; I can do nothing without sin: and, as one expresseth it, my repentance wants to be repented of, and my tears to be washed in the precious blood of my dear Redeemer; our best duties are as so many splendid sins. Before ye can speak peace to your hearts, ye must not only be sick of your original and actual sins; but ye must be made sick of your righteousness, of all your duties and performances. There must be a deep conviction before ye can be brought out of your self-righteousness; it is the last idol that is taken out of our heart, the pride of our heart will not let us submit to the righteousness of Jesus Christ. But if ye never felt that ye had no righteousness of your own; if ye never felt the deficiency of your own righteousness ye can never come to Jesus Christ. There are a great many now that may say, well, we believe all this; but there is a great difference betwixt talking and feeling. Did ye ever feel the want of a dear Redeemer? Did ye ever feel the want of Jesus Christ upon the account of the deficiency of your own righteousness? And can ye now say from your heart "Lord, thou mayest justly damn me for the best duties that ever I did perform;" if ye are not thus brought out of self, ye may speak peace to yourselves, but yet there is no peace.

But then before ye can speak peace to your souls there is one particular sin ye must be greatly troubled for; and yet I fear there are few of you think what it is; it is the reigning, the damning sin of the Christian world; and yet the Christian world seldom or never think of it; and pray what is that? It is what most of you think ye are not guilty of, and that is the sin of unbelief; before we can speak peace to your heart, ye must be troubled for the unbelief of your heart; but can it be supposed that any of you are unbelievers here in this churchyard, that are born in Scotland, in a reformed country that go to church every Sabbath? Can any of you that receive the sacrament once a year? (O that it were administered oftener.) Can it be supposed that you that had tokens for the sacrament; that you that keep up family prayer, that any of you do not believe on the Lord Jesus Christ? I appeal to your own hearts, if ye would not think me uncharitable, if I doubted whether any of you believed in Christ; and yet I fear, upon examination, we should find that most of you have not so much faith in the Lord Jesus Christ as the devil himself. I am persuaded the devil believes more of the Bible than most of us do; he believes the divinity of Jesus Christ, that is more than many that call themselves Christians do; nay, he believes and trembles, and that is more than thousands among us do. My friends, we mistake an historical faith for a true faith wrought in the heart by the Spirit of God. Ye fancy ye believe, because ye believe there is such a book as we call the Bible, because ye go to church; all this ye may do, and have no true faith in Christ. Merely to believe there was once such a person as Christ, merely to believe there is such a book called the Bible, will do you no good, more than to believe there was such a man as Caesar or Alexander the Great. The Bible is a sacred depository: what thanks have we to give to God for these lively oracles! But yet we may have these, and not believe in the Lord Jesus Christ. My dear friends, there must be a principle wrought in the heart by the Spirit of the living God. Did I ask you how long it is since ye believed in Jesus Christ,

I suppose most of you would tell me, ye believed in the Lord Jesus Christ, as long as ever ye remember; ye never did disbelieve; then ye could not give me a better proof that ye never yet believed in Jesus Christ, unless ye were sanctified early from the womb; for they that believe in Christ, know there was a time when they did not believe in Jesus Christ. You say you love God with all your heart, soul, and strength; if I were to ask you, how long it is since ye loved God, ye would say, as long as ye can remember; ye never hated God; ye know no time when there was enmity in your heart against God; then unless ye were sanctified very early, ye never loved God in your life. My dear friends, I am more particular in this, because it is a most deceitful delusion, whereby so many people are carried away, that they believe already. Therefore it is remarkable of Mr. Marshall giving account of his experiences, he had been working for life, he had ranged all his sins under the ten commandments and then coming to a minister, asked him the reason why he could not get peace; the minister looked to the catalogue, "Away, says he, I do not find one word of the sin of unbelief in all your catalogue." It is the peculiar work of the Spirit of God to convince us of our unbelief, that we have got no faith. Says Jesus Christ, "I will send the Comforter; and when he is come, he will reprove the world of the sin of unbelief." Of sin, says Christ, "because they believe not on me." Now, my dear friends, did God ever show you that ye had no faith? Were you ever made to bewail a hard heart of unbelief? Was it ever the language of your heart, Lord, give me faith? Lord, enable me to lay hold on thee? Lord, enable me to call thee my Lord and my God? Did Jesus Christ ever convince you in this manner? Did he ever convince you of your inability to close with Christ, and make you cry out to God to give you faith? If not, do not speak peace to your heart; may the Lord awaken you, and give you true solid peace before you go hence and be no more!

Once more then, before ye can speak peace to your heart, ye must not only be convinced of your actual and original sin, the sin of your own righteousness, the sin of unbelief; but ye must be enabled to lay hold upon the perfect righteousness, the all-sufficient righteousness of the Lord Jesus Christ; ye must lay hold by faith on the righteousness of Jesus Christ, and then ye shall have peace. "Come," says Jesus, "unto me, all ye that are weary and heavy laden, and I will give you rest." This speaks encouragement to all that are weary and heavy laden; but the promise of rest is made to them only upon their coming, and believing, and taking him to be their God and their all. Before we can ever have peace with God, we must be justified by faith, through our Lord Jesus Christ; we must be enabled to apply Christ to our heart; we must have Christ brought home to our soul, so that his righteousness may be made our righteousness, so that his merits may be imputed to our souls. My dear friends, were ye ever married to Jesus Christ? Did Jesus Christ ever give himself to you? Did ye ever close with Christ by a lively faith, so as to feel Christ in your heart, so as to hear him speaking peace to your souls? Did peace ever flow in upon your heart like a river? Did ye ever feel that peace that Christ spoke to his disciples? I pray God he may come, and speak peace to you. These things ye must experience. I am now talking of the invisible realities of another world, of inward religion, of the work of God upon a poor sinner's heart; I am now talking of a matter of great importance; my dear hearers, ye are all concerned in it; your souls are concerned in it; your eternal salvation is concerned in it. You may all be at peace, but perhaps the devil has lulled you asleep into a carnal lethargy and security, and will endeavor to keep you there, till he get you to hell, and there ye will be awakened; but it will be dreadful to be awakened, and find yourselves so fearfully mistaken, when the great gulf is fixed, when ye will be calling to all eternity for a drop of water to cool your tongue, and shall not obtain it.

Give me leave then to address myself to several sorts of persons; and O may God, of his infinite mercy, bless the application. Some of you perhaps can say, through grace we can go along with you; blessed be God we have been convinced of our actual sins; we have been convinced of original sin; we have been convinced of self-righteousness; we have felt the bitterness of unbelief, and, through grace, we have closed with Jesus Christ; we can speak peace to our hearts, because God hath spoken peace to us. Can ye say so? Then I will salute you as the angels did the women the first day of the week; All hail, fear not ye, my dear brethren; ye are happy souls; ye may lie down and be at peace indeed, for God has given you peace; ye may be content under all the dispensations of providence; for nothing can happen to you now, but what shall be the effect of God's love to your soul: ye need not fear what fightings may be without, seeing there is peace within. Have ye closed with Christ? Is God your friend? Is Christ your friend? Then look up with comfort; all is yours, and ye are Christ's, and Christ is God's; every thing shall work together for your good; the very hairs of your head are numbered; he that toucheth you, toucheth the apple of God's eye. But then, my dear friends, beware of resting on your first conversion: ye that are young believers in Christ, ye should be looking out for fresh discoveries of the Lord Jesus Christ every moment: ye must not build upon your past experiences; ye must not build upon a work within you; but always come out of yourselves to the righteousness of Jesus Christ without you: ye must be always coming as poor sinners to draw water out of the wells of salvation; ye must be forgetting the things that are behind, and be continually pressing forward to the things that are before. My dear friends, ye must keep up a tender, close walk with the Lord Jesus Christ. Many of us lose our peace by our untender walk. Something or other gets in betwixt Christ and us, and we fall into darkness; something or other steals our heart from God, and this grieves the Holy Ghost, and the Holy Ghost leaves us to ourselves. Let me, therefore, exhort you that have peace with God, to take care that ye do not lose this peace. It is true, if ye are once in Christ, ye cannot finally fall from God; "there is no condemnation to them that are in Christ Jesus;" but if ye cannot fall finally, ye may fall foully, and may go with broken bones all your days. Take care of backsliding for Jesus Christ's sake. Do not grieve the Holy Ghost; ye may never recover your comfort while ye live. O take care of going a gadding and wandering from God, after ye have closed with Jesus Christ. My dear friends, I have paid dear for backsliding. Our hearts are so cursedly wicked, that if ye take not care, if ye do not keep up a constant watch, your wicked hearts will deceive you, and draw you aside. It will be sad to be under the scourge of a correcting father; witness the visitation of Job, David, and other saints in scripture. Let me, therefore, exhort you that have peace to keep a close walk with Christ. I am grieved with the loose walk of those that are Christians, that have had discoveries of Jesus Christ; there is so little difference betwixt them and other people, that I can scarce know which is the true Christian. Christians are afraid to speak for God; they run down with the stream; if they come into worldly company, they will talk of the world, as if they were in their element. This ye would not do when ye had the first discoveries of Christ's love; ye could talk then of Christ's love for ever, when the candle of the Lord shone upon your soul. The time has been when ye had something to say for your dear Lord; but now ye can go into company, and hear others speaking about the world bold enough, and ye are afraid of being laughed at, if ye speak for Jesus Christ. A great many people have grown conformists now in the worst sense of the word; they will cry out against the ceremonies of the church, as they may justly do; but then ye are mighty fond of ceremonies in your behavior; ye will conform to the world, which is a great deal worse; many will stay till the devil bring up new fashions. Take care then not to be conformed to the world. What have Christians to do with the world? Christians should be singularly good, bold for their Lord, that all that are with you may take notice that ye have been with Jesus. I would exhort you to come to a settlement in Jesus Christ, so as to have a continual abiding of God in your heart. We go a building on our faith of adherence, and lose our comfort; but we should be growing up to a faith of assurance, to know that we are God's, and so walk in the comfort of the Holy Ghost and be edified. Jesus Christ is now much wounded in the house of his friends. Excuse me in being particular; for, my friends, it grieves me more that Jesus Christ should be wounded by his friends than by his enemies. We cannot expect any thing else from deists; but for such as have felt his power to fall away, for them not to walk agreeably to the vocation wherewith they are called, by these means we bring our Lord's religion into contempt; to be a by-word among the heathen. For Christ's sake, if ye know Christ, keep close by him; if God hath spoken peace, O keep that peace, by looking up to Jesus Christ every moment. Such as have peace with God, if ye are under trials, fear not, all things shall work for your good; if ye are under temptations, fear not; if he has spoken peace to your heart, all these things shall be for your good.

But what shall I say to you that have not peace with God; and these are perhaps the majority of this congregation; it makes me weep to hear of it. Most of you, if you examine your heart, must confess that God never yet spoke peace to you; ye are children of the devil if Christ is not in you; if God has not spoken peace to your heart, poor soul, what a cursed condition are you in? I would not be in your case for ten thousand thousand worlds! Why? Ye are just hanging over hell. What peace can ye have when God is your enemy, when the wrath of God is abiding upon your poor soul? Awake then, ye that are sleeping in a false peace; awake, ye careless professors, ye hypocrites that go to church, receive the sacrament, read your Bibles, and never felt the power of God upon your heart: ye that are formal professors, ye that are baptized heathens, awake, awake, and do not rest on a false bottom. Blame me not for addressing myself to you; indeed it is out of love to your soul. I see ye are lingering in your Sodom, and wanting to stay there: but I come to you as the angel did to Lot, to take you by the hand. Come away, my dear brethren, fly, fly, fly for your lives to Jesus Christ; fly to a bleeding God, fly to a throne of grace: and beg of God to break your heart: beg of God to convince you of your actual sins; beg of God to convince you of your original sin; beg of God to convince you of your self-righteousness; beg of God to give you faith, and to enable you to close with Jesus Christ. O you that are secure, I must be a son of thunder to you; and O that God may awaken you, though it be with thunder. It is out of love indeed that I speak to you. I know, by sad experience, what it is to be lulled asleep with a false peace. Long was I lulled asleep; long did I think myself a Christian, when I knew nothing of the Lord Jesus Christ.

I went perhaps further than many of you do; I used to fast twice a week; I used to pray sometimes nine times a day; I used to receive the sacrament constantly every Lord's day; and yet I knew nothing of Jesus Christ in my heart. I knew not I must be a new creature. I knew nothing of inward religion in my soul. And perhaps many of you may be deceived, as I a poor creature was; and therefore it was out of love to you indeed that I spake to you. O, if ye do not take care a form of religion will destroy your soul: ye will rest in it, and will not come to Jesus Christ at all: whereas these things are only the means, and not the end of religion; Christ is the end of the law for righteousness to all that believe.

O then awake, ye that are fettered in your lees; awake ye church professors; awake, ye that have got a name to live, that are rich and think that ye want nothing, not considering that ye are poor and blind, and naked; I counsel you to come and buy of Jesus Christ gold, white raiment and eye salve. But I hope there are some that are a little wounded. I hope God does not intend to let me preach in vain. I hope God will reach some of your precious souls, and awaken some of you out of your carnal security. I hope there are some that are willing to come to Christ, and beginning to think that they have been building upon a false foundation. Perhaps the devil may strike in, and may bid you despair of mercy; but fear not: what I have been speaking to you, is only out of love to you, is only to awaken you, and let you see your danger. If any of you are willing to be reconciled to God, God the Father,

Son, and Holy Ghost is willing to be reconciled to you. O then, though ye have no peace as yet, come away to Jesus Christ; he is our peace; he is our peace-maker: he has made peace betwixt God and offending man. Would you have peace with God? Away then to God, through Jesus Christ, who has purchased peace. The Lord Jesus hath shed his heart's blood for this; he died for this; he ascended into the highest heavens, and is now interceding at the right hand of God. Perhaps ye think there will be no peace for you. Why so? Because ye are sinners; because ye have crucified Christ, ye have put him to open shame, ye have trampled under foot the blood of the Son of God. What of all this? yet there is peace for you. Pray what did Jesus Christ say to his disciples, when he came to them the first day of the week? The first word he said was "Peace be unto you. He showed them his hands and his feet and said, Peace be unto you." It is as much as if he had said, fear not, my disciples; see my hands and my feet, how they have been pierced for your sake; therefore fear not. How did Christ speak to his disciples. Go tell my brethren, and tell broken-hearted Peter in particular, that Christ is risen, that he has ascended unto his father and your father, to his God and your God. And after Christ rose from the dead, he came preaching peace with an olive-branch of peace in his mouth, as Noah's dove, "My peace I leave with you." Who were they? They were the enemies of Christ as well as we; they were deniers of Christ once as well as we. Perhaps some of you have backslidden and lost your peace, and ye think ye deserve no peace; and no more ye do: but then

God will heal your backslidings, he will love you freely. As for you that are wounded, if you are made willing to come to Christ, come away. Perhaps some of you want to dress yourselves in your duties, that are but rotten rags. No, ye had better come naked, as you are; for ye must throw aside your rags, and come in your blood. Some of you may say, we would come but we have a hard heart: but ye will never get it soft till you come to Christ; he will take away the heart of stone, and give you a heart of flesh; he will speak peace to your soul: though ye have betrayed him, yet he will be your peace. Shall I prevail upon any of you this morning to come to Jesus Christ! There is a great multitude of souls here; how shortly must ye all die, and go to judgment; even before night, or tomorrow's night, some of you may be buried in this churchyard. And how will ye do if ye be not at peace with God! if the Lord Jesus Christ has not spoken peace to your heart. If God speak not peace to you here, ye will be damned for ever. I must not flatter you; my dear friends, I will deal sincerely with your souls. Some of you may think I carry things too far: but indeed when ye come to judgment, ye will find this true, either to your eternal damnation or comfort. May God influence your hearts to come to him! I am not willing to go away without persuading you. I cannot be persuaded but God may make use of me as a means of persuading some of you to come to the Lord Jesus Christ. O did you but feel the peace which they have that love the Lord Jesus Christ. "Great peace have they," says the Psalmist, "that love thy law, nothing shall offend them." But there is no peace to the wicked. I know what it is to live a life of sin. I was obliged to sin to stifle conviction. And I am sure this is the way many of you take; if ye get into company, ye drive off conviction. But ye had better go to the bottom at once; it must be done, your wound must be searched, or ye must be damned. If it were a matter of indifference, I would not speak one word about it: but ye will be damned without Christ; he is the way, he is the truth, and the life. I cannot think you should go to hell without Christ. How can ye dwell with everlasting burnings? How can ye abide the thought of living with the devil for ever? Is it not better to have some soul trouble here, than to be sent to hell by Jesus Christ hereafter? What is hell but to be absent from Christ? If there were no other hell, that would be hell enough. It will be hell to be tormented with the devil for ever. Get acquaintance with God then, and be at peace. I beseech you as a poor worthless ambassador of Jesus Christ, that ye would be reconciled to him. My business this morning, the first day of the week, is to tell you that Christ is willing to be reconciled to you. Will any of you be reconciled to Jesus Christ? Then, he will forgive you all your sins; he will blot out all your transgressions. But if ye will go on and rebel against Christ, and stab him daily; if ye will go on and abuse Jesus Christ, the wrath of God, ye must expect, will fall upon you. God will not be mocked; that which a man soweth, that shall he also reap. And if ye will not be at peace with God, God will not be at peace with you. Who can stand before God when he is angry. It is a dreadful thing to fall into the hands of an

angry God. When the people came to apprehend Christ,
they fell to the ground when Jesus said, I am he: and if
they could not bear the sight of Christ when clothed with
the rags of mortality, how will they bear the sight of him,
when he is on his Father's throne? Methinks I see the poor
wretches dragged out of their graves by the devil, methinks
I see them trembling, calling out to the hills and rocks
to cover them. But the devil will say, come, I will take
you away; and then they will stand trembling before the
judgment seat of Christ. They shall appear before him to
see him once, and hear him pronounce that irrevocable
sentence. "Depart from me, ye cursed." Methinks I hear
the poor creature saying, Lord, if we must be damned, let
some angel pronounce the sentence. No, the God of love,
Jesus Christ, will pronounce it. Will ye not believe this?
Do not think I am talking at random, but agreeably to the
scriptures of truth. If ye do then show yourselves men, this
morning go away with full resolution, in the strength of
God, to cleave to Christ. And may ye have no rest in your
soul till ye rest in Jesus Christ. I could still go on, for it is
sweet to talk of Christ. Do ye not long for the time when
ye shall have new bodies, when they shall be immortal,
and made like Christ's glorious body, and then they will
talk of Jesus Christ for evermore. But it is time perhaps
for you to go and prepare for your respective worship,
and I would not hinder any of you. My design is to bring
poor sinners to Jesus Christ. O that God may bring some
of you to himself. May the Lord Jesus now dismiss you
with his blessing; and may the dear Redeemer convince

you that are unawakened, and turn the wicked from the evil of their way. And may the love of God that passeth all understanding fill your hearts. Grant this, O Father, for Christ's sake, to whom, with thee and the blessed Spirit, be all honor and glory, now and for ever more. *Amen.*

NOTES

NOTES

NOTES

MAN'S QUESTIONS & GOD'S ANSWERS

Am I accountable to God?
"Every one of us shall give account of himself to God." (Romans 14:12).

Has God seen all my ways?
"All things are naked and opened unto the eyes of Him with whom we have to do." (Hebrews 4:13).

Does He charge me with sin?
"The Scripture hath concluded all under sin." (Galatians 3:22).
"All have sinned." (Romans 3:23).

Will He punish sin?
"The soul that sinneth, it shall die." (Ezekiel 18:4).
"For the wages of sin is death." (Romans 6:23).

Must I perish?
"God is not willing that any perish, but that all should come to repentance." (2 Peter 3:9).

How can I escape?
"Believe on the Lord Jesus Christ, and thou shalt be saved." (Acts 16:31).

Is He able to save me?
"He is able also to save them to the uttermost that come unto God by Him." (Hebrews 7:25).

Is He willing?
"Christ Jesus came into the world to save sinners." (1 Timothy 1:15).

Am I saved on believing?
"He that believeth on the Son hath everlasting life." (John 3:36).

Can I be saved now?
"Now is the accepted time; behold, now is the day of salvation." (2 Corinthians 6:2).

As I am?
"Him that cometh to Me I will in no wise cast out." (John 6:37).

Shall I not fall away?
"Him that is able to keep you from falling." (Jude 24).

If saved, how should I live?
"They which live should not henceforth live unto themselves, but unto Him which died for them." (2 Corinthians 5:15).

What about death, and eternity?
"I go to prepare a place for you; that where I am, there ye may be also." (John 14:2, 3).